Beneath the Ice:
Am Anthology of
Contemporary
Icelandic Poetry

D1714673

BENEATH THE ICE:

AN ANTHOLOGY OF

CONTEMPORARY ICELANDIC POETRY

EDITED BY

HELEN MITSIOS

Talisman House, Publishers • 2014
Northfield, Massachusetts

Manufactured in the United States of America

14 15 7 6 5 4 3 2 1 FIRST EDITION

Book designed by Samuel Retsov

Published in the United States of America by
Talisman House, Publishers
P.O. Box 102
Northfield, Massachusetts 01360

ISBN: 978-1-58498-112-1

ACKNOWLEDGMENTS

My gratitude to friends and colleagues whose support and encouragement has meant so much to me during the time I prepared this book – and other times in between: Aðalbjörg Baldursdóttir, Charles Borkhuis, Dr. Stanley Boylan, Barbara Braathen, Beverly Brockway, Karen Callahan, Dr. Edward Carlos, Sophie Cerda, Dr. Paul Cook , Brenda Coultas, Candee Brierley, Dr. Howard C. Cutler, Norman Dubie, Dr. Ira Gold, Lynn Goldberg, Björg Haraldsdóttir, Dr. Jules Heyman, Keiko Imai, Dr. Archer Irby, Dr. Alan Kadish, the Kliot family, Lisa Krug, Karrie Lawlor, W.S. Lewis, Marie-Elizabeth Mali, David McCall, Patricia Moya, Patrick J. O'Connell, Dr. Leon Perkal, Dr. Carmen Schuster, Hitomi Shimada, Masahiko Shimada, Borghildur Sigurbergsdóttir, and Pamela Stewart. Thank you to my husband, Tony Winters, for everything.

A special note of thanks to the Reykjavik Academy and Touro College for their on-going support.

The poetry in this book is translated by Sola Bjarnadóttir-O'Connell
except where otherwise indicated.

CONTENTS

Preface

PREFACE

In Iceland, the word for poet is still *skáld,* which dates back centuries. This small island of 325,000 people settled by Norsemen and Celts in the 9th and 10th centuries, makes every effort to nurture traditions, especially literary ones. Old Norse manuscripts and writings dating back to the early 11th century are carefully preserved and studied at the University of Iceland.

Poetry has been revered since long before it was written down. *Skálds* and minstrels were often nomads who travelled around Iceland offering to recite tales of famous battles, glorified kings and rulers, as well as ancient traditional poetry such as The Edda and Völuspá, in exchange for food and shelter. An example are the sagas of Norwegian King Harald Fairhair (A.D. 890 - 930) describing the fierce wars with his rival King Gandalf, which led to the settling of Iceland. Indeed, this saga inspired J.R.R. Tolkien, who named his wizard Gandalf.

Much of contemporary poetry speaks of cultural heritage and is based on personal experiences of daily life, be it in the city or countryside. The poetry is also primal and cryptic, stark and straightforward, cosmological and folkloric. It is about nature and the seasons: the harsh life of rural Iceland, long winter nights resplendent with the magic of the aurora borealis, and summer nights in which sheep roam in plush, fairy-tale meadows, free of natural predators found in other places.

Though there are contemporary poets who write in the mode of surrealistic, experimental and investigative poetry, most contemporary poets fall into the "romantic" genre, with nature demonstrating its power over man, and with the Eternal, rather than the transient, explored. Nature features prominently in poetry, and Icelanders often have ambivalent feelings about nature, wanting to either immerse themselves in its beauty or run away from its particular harshness. It is exceedingly powerful, bringing death-dealing storms that seem to arise from nowhere, long spells of darkness or brilliant ethereal light, and active volcanoes like Eyjafjallajokull that erupted in 2010.

Poetry has both cultural and governmental support in Iceland. Ancient as well as modern poetry is required reading from elementary school through high school. There are numerous government grants and prizes awarded to poets, and the general public attends poetry readings in local venues like libraries, cafes, and universities. Many of the poets in this collection are familiar faces in Iceland.

They are widely read and published, and have found a receptive audience in Scandinavia and Europe, and will hopefully soon find the same in the United States and Canada. With gratitude to all the exceptional poets and translators who helped to bring this collection to life, I am especially happy to include, among the excellent translators, my friend Sola Bjarnadóttir-O'Connell, winner of the 2013 Leif and Inger Sjöberg Translation Award. Sola is a gifted translator who seems to know more words in the English language than anyone I've met. Hence, I won't be challenging her to a game of Scrabble any time soon.

Icelandic poetry has always been fundamental to the culture as a source of identity, solace, and wonderment. The poets in this collection are the keepers of this tradition, the chroniclers of the present, and the *skálds* of tomorrow's sagas.

—Helen Mitsios

GYRÐIR ELÍASSON

IN THE DEEP

When the lakes freeze over, life continues
beneath the ice, though most think there is no
life there anymore

When the snow blows over the sheet of ice
small fish bustle beneath
in underwater forests,
with gleaming eyes
in the snow-lit dusk

Every night
while we sleep

SIDE BY SIDE

This sliver of a wall
between life and death
like a partition of
Japanese silk paper
torn in places
transparent

SHADOW OF THE MIDSUMMER HEDGE
for pharmacists

Abandoned
subdued
I lie down to rest
pulling the black sky
over me

THE DEEPEST LOW

When the darkness breathes on the windowpane
when a cold hand caresses the forehead
when the light does not turn on

THE CEMETERY ON A BRIGHT SUMMER DAY

A white ambulance drives
slowly on the asphalt
paths between the graves

As if it were still possible
to save anyone

THE LONER'S UNKNOWN

One never knows
what waits
around the corner
—love or death

The thing about death
is rather certain
further ahead in
time

But one day
while walking around
one either
gets hit
by a car
or meets a woman

Nothing in-between
unless the woman is driving the car.

MESSAGE TO THE NEXT MAN

Release it, the cry of anguish
that is hidden behind the calm demeanor
and the secure grip of the every day
no one can hear anyway.

A CUT IN THE SELF

When he was washing his hands
he suddenly felt like he didn't know
these hands, they were another man's hands.
He didn't dare look
in the mirror

ACCESS

Endless supply
of skeleton keys
to happiness;
few fit the lock
when it counts;
and perhaps there is no lock
rather only a hasp
that suddenly pops
open

But perhaps there is
not even a door

VISION OF THE FUTURE

Darkness falls
by the window. I see
its feathered body in
the faint light from the lamp,
how it
glistens black like coal.
One black feather
wafts in with the breeze.
I dip it into
the inkwell and
write a few words
about the sun, a few
general words about
the cooling of the sun

LINDA VILHJÁLMSDÓTTIR

HEKLA VOLCANO

drop of blood
splinter of bone
patch of skin
lock of hair

fracture of a nail
dust from a fire
that broke out last year
but went out this year

I send you a ghost

Translated by Sigurður Á. Magnússon

RHAPSODY

the word
in the beginning

then came high tide
then came low tide

and now we hear the murmur
in the distance

forceful and heavy

Translated by Sigurður Á. Magnússon

WEATHER

there was bitter frost
as I recall the previous days
and northern lights I remember
and then it began to rain

and now it has rained
for five consecutive days
and five nights my god
I am exhausted

and this story about twenty horses
stuck on an islet in White River at high tide
impending danger and a clog in North River
would be nicer in the form of frost report

the horses on the islet
the ice-bound river
and northern light

Translated by Sigurður Á. Magnússon

MORNING POEM

I am made of
light and air

above me
a gliding sea bird

beneath me
a line from a poem

the sea
is shining bright

Translated by Sigurður Á. Magnússon

THE SEA

I

tonight
he is a smooth god

runs
his heavenly fingers

through my hair
as I fall asleep

II

rising
at midnight

runs
his flaming tongue
over me

and
wakes me

III

heaving
and drowsy

a load thrusting
back and forth

into the small
hours

IV

fierce
at noon

fierce
and hurls me down

dives into me
beak and claw

HAPPINESS

now I finally know
my love

that our happiness
is like an eiderdown

that floats
in the air between us

JÓN KALMAN STEFÁNSSON

UNTITLED

It's storming. The wind whirls the snowdrifts about,
shakes up the world,
it pounds dully in the mountains.
The weather changes everything here,
snowstorm and cold draw us together
and lengthens the distance between people.
Other than the two of them,
there's no one on the road.
What would a person be searching for
outside in this kind of weather except death?

THE JOURNEY

If the devil has created
anything in this world
besides money,
then it is a snowstorm
in the mountains

ÓFEIGUR SIGURÐSSON

BISCAYNE BAY

Mighty is your strength
Mexico bay
silvery coins alive in the deep

tides & thunder
sun of changes
send mail subs
with warm wares

when seahorses snarling
after glacial rivers accept
receipts for parcels
& infants in saddle
bags gnaw on leather

swimming
swimming over the bottom
frozen seas over leaky barges
by dahlia covered banks

half buried ship of gold & tugs
rapidly finger flick
coins ashore

–V–

Sesailes de géantl'empêchent de marcher
                          – Baudelaire

The Albatross
is called Giant Sea Swallow by its kin
& and better kin is hard to find

than an Albatross
this long armed farmer's son of the sky
who closely examines ships and loads

the outlaw down on the ground
heir of shame
this overgrown Sea Swallow

poet surfs the clouds
wanders alone
smearing guano on the
city's cornerstones

– VII –

Sunshiny state fiery skies above an
abandoned city – small houses huddle
along wide avenues take your time

brother & there is ample emptiness
in this old vision

take your time brother
there is ample space
you are all good people

& cars sit on their butts
idling outside the window-
less house they are sun
burned like cotton picking men
in the fields

– IX –

& may have a tendency
to jump with dispatched
governors to charm
the girls on Miami beach

with words & thoughts
on rollerblades

about sundrenched sandy shores
forgotten things & collecting cans
on the bay alligators in the reeds
& hedgehogs in the fens

by geothermal pipes in the valleys of
Árnes county where a snipe is
startled by the tiniest rustle

GERÐUR KRISTNÝ

HOLE IN THE ICE

Drift ice in your eyes
hoarfrost in your heart

your hands
untamed sled dogs

above us
a moon poises
amid stars

target
surrounded by holes
made by darts that strayed

Translated by Sigurður Á. Magnússon

THANKS

The gifts grow
ever more original

wake up half giddy
at the sob from another's throat

This time
the sending has
been delivered

in one corner
of the room

a ghost with sad eyes

Translated by Sigurður Á. Magnússon

SUMMER POEM

In midsummer
the way between our homes
is blocked

the streets snowed up
and neither of us
wants to be the first
to clear away the snow

I remember that you were
not too keen on toil

and I have always
been fond of
snow

Translated by Sigurður Á. Magnússon

NORTH

Slow as sperm whales
we glide through the gloom
which is white
here on the heath

It holds fast to its own
conceding only
one post at a time

For an instant they flash
on the side of the road
like the little girl's matches
in the fairytale
lighting us
until we return
to the hole in the ice
to breathe

Translated by Victoria Cribb

NIGHT

As you fall asleep
your arms slide apart
no shelter there for me now
the hatches burst
and the sea breaks through

I sink
through a thousand fathoms
not one of which
enfathoms me

Slowly the seabed
subsides
beneath the weight of my sleep

Foreboding heads my way
soon it will glide
into my dream

like a visitation

Translated by Victoria Cribb

TROY

Battlements rise against
the blind sky
The gods have turned
their backs on me
they incite against me
a mighty army
a frenzied throng
of darkness

Skin stretched over
the heel's hot blood

I whet my weapon
on the bones of my foes
then hack off the heel

Draw my knife as the sun sets
sleep now, I'll hew you a horse

Translated by Victoria Cribb

ÆGISSÍÐA

Oyster catcher scurrying
over the sand
made by the master's hand
—like you

And now it is said
you have gone
to a better place

I doubt that
for there was nothing wrong
with this one until now
when the grasses huddle
fearfully on the bank

thousand fingers invoking God

Translated by Sigurður Á. Magnússon

LANGANES

We sat in the black bay
open sea to the east
home field flecked with sheep
sky with high-flying wings

Then came the fog
veiling mountain, sky and dog
you went before me
into the vanished house

I should probably
have knelt in prayer

given thanks for this day
but who was I
to interrupt God

the many-voiced whisperer
of the moor?

Translated by Victoria Cribb

TRIUMPH

The farmer drives gloating
through the district
vixen dead on the hood

He laid siege to her lair
in his jeep
so the animal smelled
the stench of petrol
not man

No one mentions
Achilles or Hector
and I know how to
hold my tongue

Translated by Victoria Cribb

KRISTÍN SVAVA

NIGHT PORTERS

the steam inside the window panes is a thick mud
like tar the sweat pours out of those
who still haven´t hooked up
arm in arm with the night and the coming day
here we do our duty and our nails rattle on the glasses
and the rock music trembles in locks of hair plastered to the temples
the house is bobbing up and down it takes a dive into the valleys and rises on
    the peaks
black towering flammable walls of sea water
sea sick men and full to the brim walk the plank step by step across
the rising falling floor my hand on the wet back of a shirt and flesh underneath
warm flesh underneath the shirt wet from beer and sweat
helpless men lose their ground and disappear quickly down the staircase
but we rock with the waves
shaking fumbling for something firm with our damp hands clasping
windowsills, glasses and one another wet and sweaty one another

UNTITLED

But my dear little heart
don't spill from a shot glass on the grave
to manufacture meaning
where there is nothing but silence

Don't think about the National Radio tape collection
about films slowly fading, dusty thumbscrews
bones of men women and hermaphrodites
about beacons that light
the way home
don't think of sniffling sponge cakes
and wakes, don't think of heritage
concealed in the ornate is the snake pit below you
—what should I do about my neighbor's decaying heart?

No rather think of burning barrels of secret documents

Police officer! Should I also burn this?
Yes my boy

about museums consumed by fire
flaming beacons
think of empty pages
and lust

United we crawl
divided we eke by
and why are we here
if not to deride what is wrongly holy
(procreate and rot)

Think of the glass
and its content
and how good it will be
when it gleefully sails down to your belly
when you pour it on the fire

I HAVE MY DOUBTS ABOUT KARL BLÖNDAL

I have my doubts about Karl Blöndal.
Why does he never receive letters
and who is this Haraldur Jónsson
who has no name plate in the building?

They said nothing about this in the manual.

I am suspicious of Karl Blöndal.
There is clearly a heartbeat in the doormat
somewhere behind this city
unearthly desires share a toast
and sharpen their claws until sunset.
When it gets dark the dogs start barking
and the woman upstairs starts crying

Rats scurry down chequered streets
with uneasy feeling in their bellies
in a night that reeks of garbage
and heavy pink blossoms.

Cats are in heat and mothers of infants
snap awake covered in sweat
fumbling for the cradle.

In a backyard, dawn is stretched thin
gradually until it is invisible.

My bravery cracks
but to be afraid is no excuse for surrender.
Here beats the heart of the universe
and I slug through it up to my knees
with one hand on the honor in my pocket.

INGUNN SNÆDAL

SUMMER LOVE

Think blue
about a flat rock
stretch it infinitely in all directions

Flowers like tiny knotted flames
by the roadside
the pink berries remind me of
the kisses we didn't share
the sea shiny like a silver brick

I tattoo an anchor on your back
you sink to the bottom

HOW A LADY PURGES

Suddenly stops talking
apologizes and slips into
the nearest bathroom locks the door and turns
on the faucet to mute the
sound leans against the wall or cabinet
aims for the sides of the toilet
so no one will hear

wipes the seat with a piece of paper flushes and
takes a tiny sip of water
and spits it out—never swallow
blots her lips rubs
her cheeks to liven up
her face shakes her head
sighs and looks in the mirror
to focus her eyes
goes back out to greet
him and his new woman

THE NIGHT IS HERE TO STAY

Where treacherous shadows and
trees claw at the raindrops
together in the dark water
lie night moon and gnats

dent from a tent
in the muddy earth

where the first of
so many black august nights

remnants of summer and sun in the grass
of us and happy laughter

other sounds belong to the night

RETURN

People my age
do not suffer love
their hearts do not break
they don't quietly expire
pale and gaunt
nothing so dramatic

They simply notice
a minor nuisance
erase numbers from
their phones
delete messages
that is why I sometimes drink
until I am seventeen
and puke on other people's floors.

FAMILY TRAITS

So sad for
you sisters
to not be tall
and thin like
your mother
my grandmother used to say

my dear
you have the shoulders
of a truck driver

is it any surprise that
my closet is void
of sleeveless dresses

AND BONES

One beautiful autumn day
my scraped white bones will be dug out
of the fragrant dark loam
mangled and maimed by the
pain I caused
to myself

because of you

my atonal voice
speaks through the ages
raspy and pleading

a loamy black rock
from a dark heart
drops onto the cold ground

but the autumn wind recalls me not
and doesn't care at all
it has found other lovers
a long time ago.

QUESTION

I know how you
sleep with me
like you don't
belong here

but how do you sleep
with her

do you belong there?

SORROW

Remember daddy
when the bird got stuck in the net
a large cold and stiff bundle

remember how the other one
circled wailing above

you pulled the net tighter
with your wet work gloves
and said
oh poor little devil

remember how my throat was so tight
when we tried to untangle him
unwinding the net over and over
while the crying bird circled above

remember when the other one finally flew away
and how relieved I was
when the cries faded into the moor

HOME

Yellow light that chases me over the mountains

lone black truck stands
abandoned by the pump
absolute stillness

two blue glasses look at me
from the cabinet above the sink

my eyes are tired
from not seeing you
the clouds hold their breath.

43

NO TV ON THURSDAYS

This is where one grew up

Like the nutty aunt
who treats yeast infection
with milk
funnel
and a few cushions under the rear

like the alcoholic farmer
fearful of work
and propensity for back pain

like the warm but aloof mother
who generally has more
sympathy with sheep than people
like the unkempt school principal
who truly believed
his wife of twelve years
didn't know he smoked

like the chubby great aunt
sunbathing naked in the garden
and giggling shy children take a long detour
around the glen.

NEW YEAR'S DAY

The winter is not white it is a westward lemony light
blue strip of ice in the sky
pink and green northern lights dragons
in a crazy chase
above the snowy plains

not cold
hot like my glance
on your parka clad back
rosy cheek

like the blood
rushing in my ears
when you suddenly squeeze my hand
through a thick wool mitten

not dark
shining bright
like the glint in your eyes

a fragile heavenly mirror.

ÞÓRDÍS BJÖRNSDÓTTIR

ON THE SHORE

He walks on the shore,
carefully inspecting the stones
so he will have something
to speak of this evening.

He picks them up, one after another,
and warms them in his palm,
then catches sight of a head in the sand.

It's the head of a little girl
staring into distance
with green eyes,
her face so white and calm.

Is she dreaming of cats?
Is she dreaming of dogs?

He sits down beside her
and arranges the stones in a ring,
forming a large circle
around them both.

"You can close your eyes now,
I will watch over you," he says,
then looks out to sea
and takes a deep breath,
hoping high tide will arrive late.

PICTURE

My love vanished in the summer heat.
I still remember how beautifully
her hair burned
as she threaded the needle,
stabbed it through his eye
and sewed in it the picture of a little girl
standing on a chair before the mirror,
plaiting her hair.

She daydreamed of women
in white dresses...

I squeeze my eyes shut
and picture her with fire in her hair
where she sits,
stroking my cheek so gently.

"And just remember not to open your eyes
or they will blind you,
or they will blind you, my love,"
she said in my ear in a whisper
and then she was gone.

CALMNESS

The grass is strangely still,
I am here to stay.

I breathe deeply listening to the insects
I am quite familiar with tonight,
and I think about old photographs,
regretting to have spent too much time
in other people's dreams.

I start humming to myself
a tune that I learned as a child,
and I reach up where I lie,
to the lowest leaves of the trees,
imagine how fine they must smell.

I hum to myself—it's a lovely tune.

Then I close my eyes and feel
how the water runs over my mind
as I fall asleep in the ashes of the moon.

A FEW SIPS OF WATER

I welcome you as I would my brother
who I drove away eleven years ago
when I had just begun wearing my green shirt
that two have owned before me.

In truth, I've always been fond of rats
though they frighten me a little
as they run along the walls in the nighttime,
but even then I long to know their secrets.

Yet I shall never give you presents
or ask about your past,
and this evening I will gather fireflies in a jar
to light the room where you'll wait for me
under a blanket of forsworn dreams
in which I drop almonds on the floor,
one after another...

I will sing you a song as I come closer
with the taste of a knife blade on my tongue,
asking myself who knows of your joys and sorrows—
do I?

I cannot tell since I am still learning to see
with the stones you gave me—
their vision obscure despite travels over seas
in which I might drown before long,
now that you've returned.
But until then, let's share these almonds before us,
swallow them with a few sips of water,
then hold our breath.

BY YOUR BED

An empty birdcage hangs from the ceiling
of the room where I stand by your bed
in my paper dress
with a threaded needle between my fingers,

and I sew into the skin of your back
the pattern of our youth
as I travel your shape
like a moon,
like a river.

Beyond I can see strangers staring at us
with the eyes of those who do not understand,
and yet one day they will eat our hearts
and treasure our bones
as if we were far more special
than they consider now.

But let me tell you—I am alive
and I will caress you as timid as you are,
and weave a blanket from my hair
to lay over you
while your breath comes to me
as from the fluttering wings of the bird,
now far away from this room,
searching for a new dwelling.

DIDDA JÓNSDÓTTIR

PASSION

I am never above suspicion
I am the axis of the unexpected
I am a passionate daughter of awareness and dreams
I am the Red Riding Hood that goes into the woods over and over again
the sleeping beauty dreaming for centuries and doesn't want to wake up
I am sadness and being and my sister's despair and ecstasy
sing with me when we are thus inclined
I am the power in electric light and chair alike
I am unspoken yet screaming
I am faith in hope and hope in faith
I am free verse yet always rhyme
rich of nothing and full of everything
I empty and replenish
I am my own antagonist
full of dare and hide everywhere
I am good when I am bad
and worst when I am best
life in life and death in death
I am written and told
painted and explained
I am requested when others want more
my father loves me and dares say it aloud
my mother feels me in her and believes in me
I am a favorite child and a bastard
result of sudden desire, an accident
I am organized mess
I am pined for
I am an impulse
I liberate the mind from the heart
I am flaming water and burning fire
I am what you are and what you don't want to be
I am unified disarray
I speak when silence is demanded

I am silent when answers are needed
I am bent and straight
I am the knife in the wound
I am the gist of the matter
I am the tears in the heart and the red lines of the limbs
I am the body inside and out
I am all it desires but don't grasp the words
I am the eddying refuse of the day and the night breeze
I am with you when you leave and always when you return
I am open on both ends but close up if empty
I have never died yet was never born
I believe in you but yet you lose to me
I am the only thing hearing your thoughts and never make you tell
when you don't want to
I am the spirit in blood and wine
I am the poison that rips and shreds
I am the edge of the knife
the open wound
umbilical cord
the last grip
but clearest of all yet invisible only to you
I am passion
all dreams and love
all flowing power
I am and I must be so
that all can be reduced to nothing
so that nothing can become itself

TODAY

No today I am not going to be
overly dramatic
and compare myself to a dried out
rose hanging upside down on a string.
No I will compare
myself to a figurehead on
a pirate ship forging ahead
with salty breasts.

THIS LIFE

I don't know
perhaps I am an ingrate
but it is not enough
for me
to meet someone
in the afterlife.
And I doubt
I will then
recall something
that I don't remember now.

BY THE DOOR

On the stoop
is the driftwood-like
corpse of my story
and the ending is
a wide open maw
demanding more.

MOMENT

I don't know how to describe this but once I stood by
a bar in my denim skirt (and it was on right) while the singer in the Pretend-
ers bought herself a drink, but I had a Guinness and whiskey
and pretended not to see her, and then I met an Irishman who had dope
and we got high while the black guy
in the Elvis costume played his blues then I had my hand
inside the Irishman's pants and then the black Elvis said:
"Ladies and Gentlemen please welcome our friend...Eric
Clapton!"
And Eric came and played his guitar and I stood there right in front
of him my denim skirt turned backwards with a joint in my left hand and an
Irish dick in my right behind my back and we...locked eyes.

ÓSKAR ÁRNI ÓSKARSSON

UNTITLED

The license plate is X 564
it is one of those
old American behemoths
the driver has rolled down
the window and nonchalantly
flicks cigarette ashes
while the car crawls down main street
the driver
has absolute control over time
and it is he who selects the music
the between-the-wars jazz
so suitable to the weather
and the rocking baby carriages on the sidewalks

UNTITLED

the old fishermen
on the harbor café sundeck
disappear behind newspapers
will soon disappear forever

UNTITLED

The streets in the auto junkyard
have been given names
Lada Street
Ford Avenue
Volkswagen Lane
those passing by the car carcasses
can't but help think
about trips down potholed roads
or asphalt sleek with rain
even red lipstick
white nylon shirts
uncertain nights
where anything can happen

UNTITLED

On the wall above the desk
hangs an old photograph
from the Highland cemetery in London
it reminds me
that every word I write
pulls me slowly
towards the end

UNTITLED

The mornings are worst
he says
before the drugs kick in
the laptop is on
he has been working on
pulling cruel words
from his mind
onto the screen

UNTITLED

The phone rings
I am addressed in Russian
(it has happened before)
the voice is a bit raspy
and I don't understand a word
it says
I say *Moscow* and the voice
says *da* and before I hang up
I ponder how many millions
reside in Moscow

UNTITLED

I have two hands
one thinks it is seventeen
the other fifty-nine
the older one reaches for stomach pills
the other pulls a lighter
out of the pocket
their relationship is generally agreeable
in spite of the age difference

UNTITLED

The first snipes are here
after flying over the ocean
it seems somehow appropriate
that they lit down just here
on the patch of grass by the
central terminal
where I take the bus
a wingless migrant

UNTITLED

One spends most of life
searching for oneself
but the best times may be
when one loses oneself
the month of May is almost gone
and I sit on a bench by the harbor
lost in a poetry book
and I don't want to be found

UNTITLED

Under the dirt everyone is equally dead
kings and pawns
he says and makes the sign of the cross
over Bobby Fisher's brand new grave

UNTITLED

Dusky June night
seagulls perched on the light posts
fragile replicas
in the china shop of the night

EINAR MÁR GUÐMUNDSSON

GUEST PLAY

I don't know if this poem was stolen
but if it was pilfered from you
it is hereby returned
along with all remains unsaid

I search long for words
    suitable for your eyes
but find none

I think:
if your eyes are words
it is uncertain that I know how to write

No, look here,
I'm no expert
in your wounds

The doctor knows so much more
about those things
but a poem knows other wounds

They visit us
every day
and are often the only guest

Translated by Anna Yates

ALCOHOLIC WOMAN

My apartment
is a trash bin for the party people
where the laughter of the drunks
has frozen in the air

As I watch, you become
a camera holding my guilt

we don't talk
because the walls that separate the rooms
are constantly between us

and wherever I go
they sneak along with me

TONES FROM THE KITCHEN OF MEMORIES

Listen.
Here are tones from the kitchen of memories.
You're back home, though they are heard much later.
Or precisely because of that
I invite you in.
We'll see what happens.

Let them move around.
I'm still talking about the memories.
And look! They're dancing in the windows of the houses,
dancing like suns,
bathed in a rosy evening glow.

Without them, we disappear
into the blackness of night
despite the shining electric lights
that point the way
out onto the highway of time
to lands which are
farther away than death.
...

A lighthouse sheds its yellowy glow
and the city lights are jewels
which God has dropped
from the clouds.

If they change into angels
I'll go with you up the mountain
and shout: May this evening go on forever,
light of the moon,
light of the world.

Look at that man
walking down the street.
His mind is a firmament

and all around him violins are being played.
I have seen the cows fly,
and seen the Almighty dancing
down a little street
in a village that never was.
...

Outlaw nights return,
the mountain crofts have vanished
like old rubber boots
and the fog carries with it
a distant singing
as it steals between the houses.
Everything else is as it was
except the ones that left.

The waves are sleeping,
I listen to the wind.
A quay bathed in blue light,
a star hiding
and the moon.

When I turn
the darkness gazes back at me.
Once there were lights,
now strange visions.

Translated by Anna Yates

And all those ifs and all those maybes,
to be or not to be.
That is why I believe in the question mark,
drown the flood of tears
and even laugh by way of protest.
Who am I and where
in among all those ifs and all those maybes...

In the beginning was the word,
and the word was a tone and the word was a picture
and it's no contradiction to be in contradiction to oneself,
for the voices of life are many
and they are heard long after
they have fallen silent

and silence talks incessantly
of all those ifs and all those maybes,
of tones and pictures, words with no beginning
for in the beginning was nothing but the word
here on earth where the belly
is as wrong as the head.

I believe in the question mark,
the quest for a connection,
a socket in God's wall
which of course has no electricity supply
or any connection to anything
but the ship of clear skies
laden with black flags
and darkness on the horizon.

That is why
I believe in the question mark,
in the circle of life
which is the last zero
in the last dollar

and nothing can save us
but all those ifs
and all those maybes,
belief within doubt
and doubt within belief,
Amen.

Translated by Anna Yates

Because it was this o'clock...
Because the weather was like that...

That's the only way I fit into the world
like the garments of a man
I don't know at all.

I don't know how they suit me,
whether they're too big
or too small.

but if they're your husband's clothes
then you're my wife
and you'll tell him so if he phones

while it's this o'clock
and the weather's like that.
...

For myself, I lie here
like a ship at the bottom of the sea.
I don't recall when I sank
but you can surely
look it up in books.

I recommend the University Library
long before these words were written
when the librarian knew every book
and had no need of a card-index
and the poet
at the desk
was thought to walk on water.

Yes, somewhere there,
on some page of some book,
you'll find my fate—

you can even pick a book
and choose a fate for me,
but if you hoist me up
you'll see my dreams
full of treasures
that have always belonged to you
in another dream,
another life.

Translated by Anna Yates

DELIRIUM BLUES

What do I know about me,
who I am,
what I mean?

I don't understand myself
but wade through intoxicated words
and images
I once saw
on a crazy television.

And then stand all alone
in the moonshine of time
but there was no wood
and no elves
just ice-flowers
taking root
behind the pupils of my eyes.

I tremble like a leaf
and the soul,
is that what's blowing through here?

Translated by Anna Yates

KRISTÍN EIRÍKSDÓTTIR

THE WAY

On the way I thought of time
and timed it while I thought of time
sat on a leather sofa and thought of the flesh
its outside and inside
I thought of time and the flesh
outside and inside
different kind of bliss
how

I lay on a tanning bed
thought of dried heads on a stick
about fire
how it consumes
about myself
I consume
thought of love connections
they burn
different kind of bliss
how

waited for the tram
the scent of leaves
thought of a trackless desert
whether it curves or falls
thought of falling
free fall
people tied with a string to a sheet
slow fall
thought of a leap
different kind of bliss
how

got off the tram

walked across a bridge
thought of strangers
about their boxes
possessions
about space between materials
whether it can be filled
whether everything is already full
thought of physical pain
how the mind gets paralyzed
about the animals
I thought about the animals in the zoo
they all have the same eyes
they are a furry frame around the same eye
one eye
different kind of bliss
how

walked through a door
thought of cannibalism
about black lips
about the taste on the tongue
elephant meat hippopotamus meat
boiled meat of an old man
about people who eat their dead children
different kind of bliss
how

thought of the hunger
of anorexia
limp cruelty
shedding clothes
that bulge out
on skinny bodies
I thought about self-hatred
gratitude
about homemade bean patties
houses that are torn down
leaking
mostly about leaking

different kind of bliss
how

walked up the stairs
all the way up
saw a lit up screen
faces beautifully painted and lit
hers that looks up
his down
thought of anger
whether it is healthy
different kind of bliss
how

heard a door open
footsteps
heard voices
mine and his
how the words became longer
pressed my face against his
tearstained cheeks smear
and said goodbye
walked downstairs
thought of sorrow
long soft sticks that
swing through the air and land
feng shui deep condition gymnastics
psychology, scented bath ego boost
different kind of bliss
how

on the way I thought about the light
how it bursts through the smallest cracks
about electricity
coursing through wires of metal and rubber
and nerves
I thought of nerves slamming together out of habit
reason for wellbeing and hunger
lust after a certain flavor

I thought of cells that vanish
pain
numbness painkillers muscle relaxants
different kind of bliss
how

thought of beauty
tiny spots of lights on leaves nature
raw nature
manufactured nature child killing
growth on groceries
inside people and asking for more
different kind of bliss
how

I thought of wax
of chemicals and flight
of desire to be made of a different material
can one change
all that flows
got on the tram sat
looked at back of heads and snaked forward
river changes its course and kills
snow that falls on places and kills
tram falling on its side
I thought about canned food
sausages in glass jars pickles
different kind of bliss
how

thought of Jesus
whether he is in tiny pieces
spread over children's duvets all over the world
whether he sings like Michael Jackson
whether he is brown or pink
whether he is also with children who need no duvets
I thought of hungry children
about food in dumpsters
whether it tastes worse

gray buildings pierce the sky
countless square black prisons
no vegetation between anywhere
got off the tram
walked on a path between buildings
thought of different ways
different kind of bliss
how

thought of gravity
about losing gravity
floating in space
the loneliness of infinity
pupils that widen in men
and fill up the hollows
seep onto the cheek
lifeless head on a lap
poison that flows
expands and pushes
head gets heavier
your frozen mien
eyes that burst

whether my death exists
whether it is far off
of material souls
flesh inside material
sausages
ghosts
about a child under a sheet with eyeholes
different kind of bliss
how

I thought about fire
burning in barrels
the people around
thought of your corpse burning
about freedom
different kind of bliss

about immolation
of blisters bursting
of the sounds
about a bang
of vocal cords expanding
inside the throat

BRAGI ÓLAFSSON

SPLENDID FEATS OF ENGINEERING

During summer
when the cruisers are sinking
in the outer harbor
one after another beneath the city-dwellers insistent admiration

the question of more surveillance of cruises becomes
more pressing
and not only more pressing but also put forward
like the question as to

why these splendid feats of engineering
these floating soirées of triumph and hope
always sink at night
always at the time our admiration is greatest

Translated by Bernard Scudder

THE EXPLORERS

When the explorers knock on the door
cold and tired
after a long journey
every human
effort will be made
to kindle the stove.
The corduroy cushions
will be brought into the sitting room
and after the stove reaches a suitable temperature
refreshments will be served
and these are refreshments worthy
of any explorer: Dry Martini
and Japanese tea;
black or green
according to taste.
They may warm themselves over this
until our curiosity
knocks on their doors: why
they sought shelter with us, what need
had driven them out of the wilderness, but then
—due to the heat from the stove—
they succumb to drowsiness and make
no reply, lean back
like setting suns,
unaccustomed to accounting for their arrival.

Translated by Bernard Scudder

WITHIN THE FRAME OF THE HOUSE

A new lodger is expected at the house,
replacing the family.
I have already decided to make friends with him:
first we greet each other with a handshake,
then I tell him about an amusing incident
which happened in the house.
And then he invites me in
although the floor is all covered with books
and no curtains over the windows.
Then I sit in the only chair I can see
and notice framed portraits of faces
some of which resemble him.
He starts apologizing for the mess
and then I have another idea which I mention to him:
that it would be fun to swap pictures,
he could have pictures of my family,
I could have some of his.
He apologizes for the mess once again.
He is expected shortly.

Translated by Bernard Scudder

HÓLL MOUNTAINS

From the horse
that is bored carrying me
I listen to the cracks in the mountains

Pull at the reins
by a black bar
and hitch up the horse to the darkness

Translated by Martin Regal

SIGFÚS BJARTMARSSON

SPRING IN THE WETLANDS

Colors bursting in light
the tiny fish is ice needle the bird soaring
the breeze is transparent the knoll is icy
the man a shadow of himself
in other words all good news.

THE EX

He still couldn't resist
and always answered the phone in the end
.he fell for the temptation to sneak to the window
and yes the taxi is just pulling up to
the door and the void was still sitting
in the backseat.

MEMORIAL AT SOUTH STREET

The liveliest tree and the trilling
rising from a woman who was deemed so birdlike
looking and light as dust in the coffin.

LANDSCAPE WITH TIME

So sunny is this valley
that by morning a tiny daylight remains
from yesterday.

So mighty are these mountains
that night shadows alone
can embrace them.

So sheltered is this dell
that hidden in the brush is a slight warmth
from bygone ages.

FROM *ZOMBIE*

10

Zombie
The garden at home is wonderful
home is best
perennial memory growth
and the spectrum of color
and the frost.

And afar
from the street wafts
one and another thousand watts
of darkness in the belly.
And steals
so quietly over the lawn
by the walls to the window
towards the black frost roses and
crazy graffiti
of the peeping toms.

And you
peek and see
this is wonderful
yes very certain –
the hermit is not at home.

27

Each portion
of new reality into the dream life
adheres to altered consciousness and
is sometimes better.

Zombie
Look at this
and now I reach for another

drunk bit of wisdom from my *hazy spirit*
and you gather more torn
velvet notes on the depth of the mind
barbed wire in the grass and caress
the colored wings of butterflies
pull out the pins
and stick them in again
gently touching needles and edges
while I discuss the importance
of knowing what one is
liberated from.

And then it helps
to realign the deceits
dust them off also the shelves
be kind to your own like an old
hunter reanimating his
stuffed birds.

Then time passes nicely
like a glittering wake
gliding downstream on
the D-side of the evening's
vinyl

and we
so pleasantly numb
surely from the beating
in the final round

Zombie
time has come
to take the course anew
the back and forth bridge that
never ends
until daybreak.

Zombie
Look at the dawn
like it is on fire
this is beautiful
and just like joy should be
and happiness too except bigger
one giant piece of darkness that burns up
like a tire shop
fully insured and bankrupt
always prepared to sear value into life
when the needful things are so
achingly broken

And somewhere
out there is a hole for me
and a hole for you Zombie
warm from the ashes of
careless ills.

ÞORSTEINN FRÁ HAMRI

SIGRÍÐUR GUÐMUNDSDÓTTIR FROM ILLUGASTÖÐUM
   b. 1811 at Vatnsendi in Vesturhóla county
   relocated to Copenhagen general prison in 1830,
   d. there April 5, 1839

Born with longing and hope
but inured to obedience:
unassuming, kind,
guileless and fearful.

A note of her worldly belongings
states: shawl with holes,
wool skirt, torn,
another, almost useless,
well-worn apron,
old blue lady's cap
with a silk pouf, damaged.

And like a symbol
of something whole, even a shelter:

a small box
where you kept green
silk twine...

A SONG OF INNOCENCE

I go to the door
determined: Now is the moment.

To resist invasions.
Keep them outside.
Stop.

And slam the door shut...
Then behind me, others open.

CHILDHOOD

Give me again
a sense

of a distant stream
a girl
a rose
and a shepherd...

Let a glimpse of her
quickly appear
and vanish

at the moment when
light strikes the wick

light,
that can be dim
very, very dim.

BREAKING SOUND

Grassy and ancient
are the fields of sorrow

and hardly anyone walking there
can avoid stepping on at least one irreplaceable
mirror of god.

CONFESSION BOOTH

Is shame the
cloud,
the veil, that hides
a smile

where an imperious, dear
memory is worshipped, adored
in regret, obduracy—and silence
of the mysterious souls

steeped in impending
sorrow?

MEGAS

ORPHEUS AND EURYDICE

Like a hammer quickly hitting anvil
rain beats on the roof
but in your quiet tear
is joy light warmth

your kind joyous magic
nourishes my spirit soul and strength
to you I will always sacrifice
my worldly goods
as long as my heart beats

Your sleep a glassful of god
offers peace in a hard fought war
is how I strive through the years
until at last I sleep in the ground

The mountain circle is drawn
in a ring around me
and outside of it is nothing
because inside I have you

But we must contend with a little snow
for a while
you resting on the slope behind the house
soon we will meet there
she was beautiful and kind
she was better than them
and when she sleeps by my side
I sleep in peace

The sun rises in the east
but sits down in the west
in the valley where I opened my eyes
is always peace and quiet

My horse's name is Blesi
we have shared so many years
I keep going but getting shorter yet
is his journey

My Blesi on the slope a pleasant
resting place is ready for you
someday I will rest with you
exhausted old disappointed man

TESTAMENT

I lovingly listen
leave to the like-minded a script
to be torn apart piece by piece
with great enjoyment

I lovingly listen
leave to the like-minded the pain
of a slow burn in a fire in spite of
having a choice

I lovingly listen
leave to the like-minded the pain of
devotion to self destruction
and to neglect more useful pursuits

I lovingly listen
leave to the like-minded a judgment
an inability to see the value of life
but pursue adoration of emptiness

I lovingly listen
leave to the like-minded the pain of
ever distrusting the good gods
and pay back in kind

I lovingly listen
and hand to the like-minded fate
of resurrecting my sad sign
I will push out soon

TWO STARS

Time flies forward pulling me behind
and I have no say in where it goes.
But I hope it thinks a little warmly of me
and in the end brings me back to you.

I once gave you a chain of gold to wrap around your neck,
lest you would forget me in the daily grind.
I watched myself in your black eyes for a while
and hoped I could stay there forever more.

Many things bother me but not the wait
because I see first in the dust how much time has gone by.
And write something all important there with my finger.
Because my night is dark and lonely and the day is on fire.

Yes and your face is painted. How clearly I recall
eyeliner and pink lips and a sunny smile.
Yes I know free is always best.
But I then pay a heavy price for the worst.

I miss you at dawn and not having you beside me
and I miss you in the daytime when the sun smiles on me.
And I miss you in the evening when darkness falls.
But I miss you most at night when the ghosts start to roam.

Then I look up and see, the two of us together up there
two stars in the blue getting closer and closer.
I remember you every minute my eyes are open,
but now when I close them I can go to find you.

ÞÓRARINN ELDJÁRN

NAILS

The nail-studded sticks
all went into the fire.

Now as I shovel the ashes
the nails reappear
free from bondage
clinking impatiently on the shovel.

Worn
and seemingly bent
but tough
and ready for anything.

FAIRY TALE

One autumn evening around 1970 I popped into
Hviids Vinstue. Aiming to warm up my insides
although the exterior
should be able to continue to withstand the north-European
chill, that the Skane prairie is so well known for. I soon
noticed an old lady, ageless sot(ess)
who sat deep in a corner sipping a drink. I thought
she looked somewhat familiar but could not place her, until she
opened her mouth and related her story.
I was the only one listening as everyone else seemed to have heard it before:
Here was no other than the child from *The Emperor's New Clothes*, and
    as you can imagine
she had not known a life of ease since falling out of favor.
Too bad that my comprehension of Danish is so limited.

IMAGINE

My neighbor, whom I often ran into at the store, had a
more powerful antennae than others and had many stories from
the great lands on other planets where only Icelandic
is the official language. The orders to us from there were
clear: Cease fishing, harness the language.
I elated my friend by telling him that I had already done that
a long time ago. Otherwise it seemed like the main occupation up there
    was like
one giant course in Icelandic for foreigners. It is going pretty well, said my
neighbor. Mao for instance is getting incredibly good. Only one man
did not take orders and clung to his own mother tongue
like a dog to a bone: John Lennon. Good for him
to always fight oppression, I thought but didn't say
anything.

SNEAKY

Sneaky clouds
cover the sun they bathe in.

Sneaky lakes
deep or shallow.

Sneaky grass
hiding in the ground.

Sneaky children
know so little yet everything.

Sneaky words
always first but show up last.

Sneaky answers
asking what the question was.

EXCELSIOR

Yellow sticks
mark a black road
in the wide open green.

Red tractor
sprouts wings
and takes
flight
over the moor.

GREAT BEGINNING

It is a great beginning to
wake up in a new place
although the hotel carries only
one star
if that is the one shining.

My wish for disturbance
I have hung on the door knob
soon a call to
breakfast will sound.
Also a great beginning
is to awaken to a new day.

Many things occurred in dreams
especially wildfires
and a peek into an old book
margins cut
into the quick of the text
so no room for comments.

They shall hereby be put forth.

ANGELICA VERSAILLICA

Early spring we came to Versailles and lay down
on a lawn in the park. In my jacket pocket I found a few
handfuls of Angelica seeds. I had
collected those the fall before at Ægissíða in Reykjavik
and not worn the jacket since. We sowed these seeds
into French soil and watered generously
with spring water from Evian on the south side of lake Geneva.
The whole summer I had dreams,
that may have been someone else's nightmare.
The palace was buried in a thicket of Nordic edible Angelica
and the sun kings couldn't see the sun. Already at the train station the air
was filled with the scent of sweet anise. Then again it also was possible that
    nothing happened.
I was able to confirm that the following spring when I passed by there again.
    But the image remains.

GLOSSARY

Ægissíða: literally means seaside and refers to a street and an area on the south sideof the Reykjavik peninsula

Langanes: a long peninsula that is located on the north east corner of Iceland, and is shaped a little like a duck. It is very desolate but beautiful

Hekla: a majestic mountain and very much a part of Icelandic lore. It is considered female. It is an active, but at the moment dormant, volcano and has been known to bring a great deal of destruction in its awesome beauty

Hóll Mountains: a peak in northern Iceland, but basically Hóll Mountain means hill or peak

Hviid's Vinstue: a Danish wine bar/pub

Skane: a section of south Sweden that has a bit of a prairie feeling. The inhabitants speak with what sounds like a Danish accent

ABOUT THE POETS

Sigfús Bjartmarsson   is known for his exceptional imagery and the wide variety of his subjects, which are frequently taken from the reality and culture of other countries.   With the book *Zombie* (1992) he established himself as one of the leading Icelandic poets today.

Þórdís Björnsdóttir   is a poet and novelist. Since 2004 she has published two novels, a collection of short stories and three books of poetry, *Hiding Behind the Curtains* (2007), *And Then Came Night* (2006), and *Love and Oranges* (2004).

Kristín Eiríksdóttir studied visual art in Iceland and Canada but has mostly devoted her time to writing. She has published three books of poetry, a collection of short stories, a novel and two of her plays have recently been staged at the National Theatre of Iceland and at the Reykjavík City Theatre.

Gyrðir Elíasson is one of Iceland's most prolific writers. *The Yellow House*, was awarded the Icelandic Literature Prize, and his most recent award is the 2011 Nordic Council Prize for Literature. His poetry collection, *Some General Words on the Cooling of the Sun,* was published in German translation in 2011.   His works have been published in translation in both Germany and France, and the short story collection *Stone Tree* was published in English in 2009.

Þórarinn Eldjárn is a writer and translator who has published a number of poetry collections, short-story collections and novels as well a translating fiction for adults and children from English and the Scandinavian languages. Among them are novels by Göran Tunström, and Lewis Carroll's *Alice in Wonderland*. His novel *The Blue Tower* has appeared in several languages, including English and French and was nominated to the IMPAC Dublin award in 2001.

Einar Már Guðmundsson is recipient of The Swedish Academy Nordic Literature Prize, 2012. He is one of the most widely translated Icelandic author born in the post-war period, a novelist, short-story writer and poet. His first collection of poetry was published in 1980, and he immediately became one of the leading voices of neorealism. His poetic diction was a bold attempt to make slang and foreign loan words legal tender in poetry, and to draw images from everyday life. He has received many awards, including the Nordic Council Prize for Literature in 1995 for *Angels of the Universe*, a novel that was later adapted into a success-ful film.

Þorsteinn frá Hamri has written seventeen books of poetry and has been nomi-nated for the Nordic Council Literature Prize four times. His most recent poetry collection *Earth Signs* was published in German by in 2011. The anthology spans Þorsteinn's fifty-year career. Among his awards are the Children's Book Literary Award for Translation, the Þorbergur Þórðarson Literary Prize, and the Icelandic Literary Prize.

Gerður Kristný has published poetry, short stories, novels, and books for chil-dren. Among her numerous awards are the Children's Choice Book Prize in 2003, the Halldór Laxness Literary Award in 2004 for her novel *A Boat With a Sail and All* and the West-Nordic Children's Literature Prize in 2010. Gerður's collection of poetry *Soft Spot* was nominated for the Icelandic Literature Prize in 2007, and she then won the prize in 2010 for her poetry book *Blóðhófnir*, which is based on the myth about Freyr from the Eddic poem *Skírnimál*.

Didda Jónsdóttir. Her first book, the poetry collection *Bad Habits and Loose Screws* was published in 1995. Since then, Didda has published two novels. She played the leading roles in the film *Stormy Weather* by French/Icelandic director Sólveig Anspach, which premiered in Cannes in 2003. Didda received the Ice-landic Edda Film Award as best actress for her role in the movie. She also played the leading role in Anspach's film *Be Right Back* in 2008.

Magnús Þór Jónsson, known as Megas, is one of the most popular poets in Ice-land. A songwriter and performer. He is widely acclaimed for his prolific and sometimes controversial works. This is the first time he's permitted his poems to be translated and published in English.

Bragi Ólafsson is the author of several books of poetry and short stories, and four novels, including *Time Off*, which was nominated for the Icelandic Literature Prize in 1999 (as was *The Pets*), and *Party Games*, for which Bragi received the DV Cultural Prize in 2004. His most recent novel, *The Ambassador*, published in English by Open Letter in 2009, was a finalist for the 2008 Nordic Literature Prize and received the Icelandic Bookseller's Award as best novel of the year.

Óskar Árni Óskarsson has published ten poetry books as well as six collections of short prose. He was co-editor of the poetry journal *Clouds*, which was published from 1990 -1994. Óskar Árni has received a number of literary prizes and nominations. In 2004 he was awarded the National Radio's Literature Prize, in 2006 he received the Jón úr Vör Poetry Prize, and he was nominated for The Icelandic Literature Prize in 2008.

Ófeigur Sigurðsson has published six books of poetry and two novels. Ófeigur is at the forefront of a poetic movement of dynamic young creative people, who have recently had a hand in reshaping the form of Icelandic poetry. He received the 2011 European Union Prize for Literature for his novel *Jón*.

Ingunn Snædal Her first book of poetry *On Hot Pavement* was published in 1995. Since then she has published two other books of poetry. *Godless Men — Thoughts About Glacial Water and Love* won Reykjavík City's poetry award, The Tómas Guðmundsson Literature Prize in 2006, and was also nominated for The Icelandic Literature Prize. Ingunn's poetry has also been published in Norwegian and German.

Jón Kalman Stefánsson is recipient of the 2011 P.O Enquist Award and his novels have been nominated three times for the Nordic Council Literature Prize. His novel, *Summer Light, Enter Night* received the Icelandic Literary Prize in 2005. His best known work is a trilogy of novels: *Heaven and Hell* (2007), *The Sorrow of Angels* (2009) and *The Heart of Man* (2011). The third and final book in the trilogy won the Icelandic Bookseller's Prize 2011. He recently won the Italian Grinzane Bottari Lattes Prize for the second installment in the trilogy.

Kristín Svava Tómasdóttir is the young rebel poet of Iceland. She published her first poems in various periodicals, and frequently participates in readings and events on the poetry scene. Her first poetry book *Tender Swear Words* received the Icelandic Booksellers' Prize in 2007. In 2011 she followed it up with the *The Barbarian Show*.

Linda Vilhjálmsdóttir is a poet, playwright and novelist. Her poetry has been included in several collections and her first poetry book *Hanging by a Thread* was published in1990, since then she has published three more, one of which (*The Ice Children*) won the DV Cultural Prize in 1993. In 2003 she published a semi-autobiographical novel: *Made-up Story.* Her plays have been staged at the Reykjavik City Theatre as well as other smaller venues.

About the Translators

Victoria Cribb is one of Icelandic literature's best-known translators into English, working with Arnaldur Indriðason, Sjón, and Gyrðir Elíasson, among others. She became interested in Iceland as a teenager and taught herself the language with a 1948 Linguaphone set. She lived, worked and studied in Reykjavík for a total of nine years and is currently finishing her Ph.D. on Old Icelandic sagas at the University of Cambridge.

Sigurður Á. Magnússon was a translator for the United Nations, and a lecturer on Old Icelandic Literature at the New School for Social Research. He has written many books, in Icelandic and English, including novels, poems, plays, travel books, memoirs, essay collections as well as translating works from Danish, English, Greek and German.

Sola Bjarnadóttir-O'Connell is recipient of the 2013 Leif and Inger Sjöberg Translation Award conferred by The American-Scandinavian Foundation. She has translated numerous articles and web content for private and official instances in Iceland, and is currently working on translations of contemporary Icelandic short stories. Originally from Iceland, Sola divides her time between New York City and Reykjavik.

Martin Regal lives in Reykjavik and has been teaching at the University of Iceland for over thirty years. His translations of *Gisli's Saga* and the *Saga of the Sworn Brothers* have appeared in Penguin editions. He has also translated numerous works of poetry and fiction.

Bernard Scudder was a poet and pre-eminent translator. Among his translated works are *Egil's Saga*, *Grettir's Saga*, and he was the editor of a five-volume compilation of skaldic poetry

Anna Yates is a writer and translator of English and Icelandic descent. Her translations include fiction and a range of books and projects about Iceland and its nature, history, and arts.

ABOUT THE EDITOR

Helen Mitsios is the editor of *Digital Geishas and Talking Frogs: The Best 21st Century Short Stories from Japan*, and *New Japanese Voices: The Best Contemporary Fiction from Japan* which was twice listed as a *New York Times Book Review* Summer Reading Selection and Editors' Choice. She is the co-author of *Waltzing with the Enemy: A Mother and Daughter Confront the Aftermath of the Holocaust*. She is recipient of the Gwendolyn Swarthout Award in Poetry and a professor of English at Touro College in New York City.

In praise of *New Japanese Voices: The Best Contemporary Fiction from Japan: The New York Times Review of Books*, listed twice as an Editors' Choice • *The New York Times Review of Books*, listed as suggested "Summer Reading" • "Ms. Mitsios has assembled an intelligent collection." —Herbert Mittgang, The *New York Times Book Review* • "The 12 writers in New Japanese Voices selected by the editor, Helen Mitsios, share a stylish insouciance – an ennui in Ray-Bans-that will remind readers of Jay McInerney, who provides the introduction." — *The New York Times Book Review*–Editors' Choice • "Mitsios assembles an impressive range of literary ambassadors. This anthology should firmly resolve debates about the vitality of Japanese fiction." —*Publishers Weekly* • "A happy marriage of contemporary Western culture with the traditional Japanese sensibility makes this story collection by young Japanese writers a worthwhile successor to a distinguished literary past. A timely and welcome debut." —*Kirkus Reviews* • "There's real energy, real humor, real life [...] that bodes well for Japanese literature as these yuppie writers grow up." — *The Washington Post Book World* • "This engaging skewing of reality shows us our own lives, as good fiction should do, in a new light." — *L.A. Style* • "It is these writers who best give non-Japanese a clear idea of what it means to be living in Japan today." —*The Japan Times*, Tokyo • "Short stories of intriguing cadence and unusual imagery from a dozen of Japan's best young writers." —*Mother Jones "Guide to the Season's Best"* • "Admirably, Mitsios sets out to prove the existence and vitality of postwar Japanese literature with this book, showcasing a new generation of writers." — *Harvard Book Review* • "Twelve writers and nine translators are gathered in the excellent collection *New Japanese Voices.*" —*The Asia Society Newsletter*

In praise of *Digital Geishas and Talking Frogs: The Best 21st Century Short Stories from Japan*: "We have in this new volume of fiction a group of fine new short stories...and read it you should." Alan Cheuse, —*SF Gate: San Francisco Chronicle* • "Great stories rewire your brain, and in these tales you can feel your mind shifting as often as Mizue changes trains at the Shinagawa station in 'My Slightly Crooked Brooch.' The contemporary short stories in this collection, at times, subversive, astonishing and heart-rending, are brimming with originality and genius." —David Dalton, author of *Pop: The Genius of Andy Warhol* • "Here are stories that arrive from our global future, made form shards of many local, personal pasts. In the age of anime, amazingly, Japanese literature thrives." —Paul Anderer, Professor of Japanese, Columbia University • "I am going to make a prediction since I really do believe that this will be true: *Digital Geishas and Talking Frogs* is going to be an important book for the next decade or so." —Will Ees, *Junbungaku: Japanese Literary News* • "*SF* takes interesting turns and shouldn't be turned aside for some of its more unconventional content (as if that wasn't reason to read it enough)." —Julianna Romanazzi, Three *Percent: A Resource for International Literature at the University of Rochester* • "Helen Mitsios has done an excellent job not only with the selection of stories but also with the way they flow from one to another, and the individual translations have been edited to maintain a cohesive yet unobtrusive "house style" that still manages to show off the individual writing style of each author. In short, *Digital Geishas* contains a good batch of stories that have benefited from solid editing. This book is a wonderful follow-up to Mitsios's earlier compilation, *New Japanese Voices*." — Kathryn Hemmann, *Contemporary Japanese Literature* blog • "Now Mitsios returns with a second collection: cause for celebration, immediate ordering, immersion in these thirteen worlds of Story." — *World Literature in Review*